All that glitters aint GOLD

A guide for every girl to be Godly Esteemed!

Sheree Braswell

Copyright © 2019 by Sheree Braswell

All rights reserved. No part of this book may be reproduced in any form on by an electronic or mechanical means, including information storage and retrieval systems, without permission in writing from the author and publisher, except by a reviewer who may quote brief passages in a review.

Cover Design: Gabriel Reed

Editors: Ellen Maze, Aretha Borden-Davis, and Dr. Martina Wade-Hill

ISBN: 9781794446984 (Paperback)

All that Glitters Ain't Gold! -- A Guide for Every Girl to be Godly Esteemed

Acknowledgements:

Dedicated to my Lord and Savior, Jesus Christ. As the apple of my eye, you make all things possible. I am so honored to serve such an awesome Heavenly Father. You healed me in so many ways and put the puzzle pieces of my life together to help me see purpose in life. All credit goes to you. I adore You and I can't wait to write many more books to bring you Glory and Honor.

To my parents, thank you for teaching me how to love myself and helping me see myself in the way God sees me. You have raised me to have standards and never looked down on me when I made mistakes along the way. Thank you for seeing the best in me and being the wonderful parents that you are. I love you!

To my Apostle, Dr. Martina Wade-Hill, thank you for being a great mentor and spiritual leader/parent. Your constant support and encouragement has been pivotal in my journey. I will never forget, at one of your events in 2015, you prophesied to me that I would write a short self-esteem book for girls. At that time, I only had a title of my book. Now four years later, it came to pass. You are amazing in every way. You have challenged me to become the young woman that I am today. I am grateful for you and our friendship and sisterhood. Also, I love that we're cousins—favorite cousins at that!

To my best friend, Amelia Allen, thank you for all the love and support you have given to me over the years. You have helped me grow and mature and taught me how to be a better friend. Thank you for believing in me and standing with me, when so many others left. Thank you for being a genuine friend.

You are someone in whom I can confide in and love. Thank you for believing in this book and the support that you have shown. Thank you for helping me in my journey when I was discovering who I am and my purpose while learning how to love myself, my body image, and so much more. You have definitely been a friend that sticks closer than a brother / sister (Proverbs 18:24).

To my family and friends, thank you for loving me and supporting me. I wouldn't be who I am today without my community. You all rock and I love you!

Dedicated to:

Every girl in the world who felt like her world was crushed and stolen, who also felt lost in it. May this book reveal to her that her safe place is in Christ and that she is highly valued. You are beautiful from head to toe and loved in every way by GOD, your Father in heaven.

Introduction

<u>Psalm 45:13</u> ESV

All glorious is the princess in her chamber, with robes interwoven with gold.

<u>Psalm 45:9</u> ESV

Daughters of kings are among your ladies of honor; at your right hand stands the queen in gold of Ophir.

Think of yourself dressed in the finest of gold going to the biggest, most extravagant ball of your life. Dressed in a sparkly gold sequined dress that reflects every available beam of light in the room! You have been invited by King Jesus to come in your very best to the finest dinner. You have this special night with the King and He has a special pure gold book for you. You may not be able to afford the book, but He paid the price and gave it to you for free! This book reveals every chapter of your life, the story is going to play through. As the host of the event, which I only charge you the price of this book to attend, I'm going to walk you through the process that Jesus gave to me. My desire is to see you whole, set free, and inspired to live your best life in Christ. I want you to feel smitten with so much love, and to finish this book full of confidence and fierceness. You are worth it. Thank you for purchasing this ticket (book) and allowing me to walk into the chapter of your life where you may need it the most. I will help you on your journey to build a healthy self-esteem. So, sit back and enjoy, because you are golden!

Chapters

1. You are Fearfully and Wonderfully Made
2. Body Image
3. Self-Esteem
4. But I Thought He Was the One!
5. Value Me
6. Declaration to Love God
7. Declaration to Love Myself
8. Declaration to Wait for Your Future Husband

Chapter 1 You are Fearfully and Wonderfully Made

According to the Bible, we are fearfully and wonderfully made (Psalm 139:14). For the longest time, I struggled in this area. I struggled to believe that God shaped me for my purpose and that how I looked was pleasing. Growing up, I was teased for my big head and I felt very insecure about it. I had a wide gap between my front teeth which caused me to despise smiling.[1] I've always had big feet, which as a young girl, I remember in the 6th grade not wanting to go roller skating because I was ashamed to say my shoe size out loud, when choosing my skates. I had bad acne breakouts that were only tamed later when I got on birth control. To top it off, I felt like my nose was shaped funny and much too big. From the crown of my head to the soles of my feet, I was very critical of myself. Daily, I rejected how God made me, and wanted to look like someone else.

---

[1] Interestingly, wearing braces fixed the gap, but eventually, it came back.

As I matured, I had no problem recognizing other girls' beauty, or even complimenting them, but I could not look at myself in the mirror and believe I was just as beautiful as they. Eventually, I realized the girls that I thought were beautiful had insecurities of their own. I saw these girls with their beautifully-applied makeup on their lovely faces; and thought they had the cutest shapes! Little did I know that these girls were insecure *without* makeup and they were dealing with issues concerning their weight.

Ever since I was little, I loved playing in my mother's makeup. By the time

I got to high school, I wore eyeliner and mascara daily. When I got to college, I broke away from the habit of applying makeup every day because I wanted to see if I could love myself naturally. It did not take me long to like the way I looked without makeup, and I thought I was beautiful that way. But at a friend's wedding in April 2016, I wore a full face of makeup. So many people commented on how beautiful I looked which made me question myself, "Am I just as beautiful without makeup?"

When I went to prom in 2010, I had a perm; after that, I went on a natural hair journey. Some of the remarks were very good from men and women of all different cultures. However, some would only tell me how beautiful I am with my hair straightened. As an African American woman, I felt it was important to embrace my natural curl pattern. I was tempted to go back to the creamy crack, during my transition period, but I am glad I hung in there. I went a long time without wearing makeup, as I worked through these issues. Around the time of Spring 2017, I went back to wearing makeup. I finally learned that it is okay to enjoy makeup and love the way it enhances one's natural beauty, but it never should be used as a cover-up for insecurities.

Ideally, we should feel that we are beautiful with and *without* makeup!

Sisters, I want to encourage you. It is tempting to judge our beauty by the opinions of others. We must know that God designed us and looks at us as being created in His image which is good. You are made in His image and likeness (Genesis 1:27). He made you perfectly for your calling and purpose. He made no mistakes in your height, body frame, facial and body features, complexion, hair texture or shoe size. He knew your ethnicity before you were born and chose it on purpose. Social media (and media, period) has brainwashed us in regards to what beauty looks like. Social media provides a way for our self-esteem to be boosted by our followers' likes and little "hearts". They love on our pictures after we get our hair done, or buy a new outfit. We focus on our social media post in the hopes of garnering some attention from others. Ever had that thought before you post a really cute picture of yourself that you knew you were going to get a lot of likes and comments on it? I will be honest, I have. But then, God told me, *daughter, you are beautiful, and the number of likes and comments doesn't determine your worth. You are worth more than rubies.* It took me a while to recognize that the attention and validation I was seeking from society would never amount to the security and validation that God says about me in His word.

The same goes to you, my beautiful sister. God says you are altogether beautiful and there is no flaw in you (Song of Solomon 4:7). So yes, honey, you are *absolutely flawless,* because God says so. How many of you can nod your head and agree that you determine your beauty by the compliments of a really fine guy? As if his opinion makes it worth the count? If this is you, you're not alone. Whenever very attractive guys were trying to talk to me, I knew I was really attractive. Their opinions mattered more than they should have. When I went to college, it seemed like I met a lot of fine guys that were physically alive (muscular), but spiritually dead. This topic will be covered a little later in this book.

My sisters, you have a purpose and a calling that God assigned before you were formed in your mother's womb. You have gifts and talents and spiritual gifts that God needs you to use without comparing to anybody else's. For the longest part of my journey, I frowned upon my purpose, because I experienced the most shame, embarrassment, and pain in the area of mental health. In 2012, God told me my purpose was to minister to the mentally oppressed. In 2015, I shared my story with my church family, close friends, and Periscope of my personal experience living with mental illness. In May 2016, for Mental Health Awareness Month, I blogged my story and shared it with the world, claiming myself as a mental health awareness advocate. I felt fulfilled in purpose, but still had lots of insecurity, comparing myself to others. I wished that my ministry could look pretty like 'Pinky Promise'.[2] As a result doors were opened when I had an

---

[2] https://www.pinkypromisemovement.com/
Founded by Heather Lindsey in 2012, "Where we strive to honor God in our lives and hearts."

opportunity to interview Heather Lindsey and her husband on my own radio show at Wayne State University. I honor Heather Lindsey for her work and her ministry. I wished that I was as prophetic as my Apostle, Dr. Martina Wade-Hill. I wished that I could see more in the spirit realm (and see angels, not the demons, lol), and be able to speak prophetically into people's lives on a keen and high level of the prophetic. Instead, I needed to understand that this is how God fearfully and wonderfully made *them* in order to add to their world. Their purposes have power and so do yours and mine!

Being fearfully and wonderfully made means embracing what God has called you to do. I know God birthed passions in your heart to fulfill for His Glory on this Earth. To walk in your call fearlessly and confidently means to know that it is unique and that you were equipped to do it, to fulfill it until the day of Christ, no matter how many people may have similar gifts and callings. You can stay in your lane and cheer others in theirs. Fulfilling your calling and purpose is not a race and there is no competition; we will all make it to the finish line if we don't quit. You must know that it's all about the one who endures to the very end, ***Matthew 24:13*** *King James*

Version (KJV) [13] But he that shall endure unto the end, the same shall be saved. I dare you to step out and do what God has called you to do. The world needs you right now. The world needs to hear your story and testimony. The world needs to hear how you overcame in Christ. The world needs to see your gifts and talents. Whether it's dancing, singing, worshipping, cooking, designing and making clothes, teaching, writing books, motivational speaking, or whatever it may be; the many things God has called people to do is limitless and He purposes us all. Your gifts, talents, looks were made to glorify God. So, I leave you, in my Tyra Banks voice, "Honey, you better work it!

Journal #1 Fearfully and Wonderfully Made

1. Write 5 affirmations on a note card and place them somewhere visible, such as your mirror, and repeat those affirmations out loud. (Ex: I am beautiful, I am smart, I am fearless, etc.)

2. What are some areas you felt insecure in. Example: your purpose, gifts, talents, and calling, physical looks? Write them down and find Scriptures

from the Holy Bible to help you overcome those insecurities.

3. What is one area you would like to change or improve in your life? Why do you want to change it? Do you think God can use that area to serve your purpose?

_____

_____

_____

_____

_____

_____

_____

Chapter 2 Body Image

Body, body, body, and body! It seems like we, in America, are an extremely visual-based society, where you can't even get a job, at times, if you're not the "right size." For the longest time, I struggled with my body image. Even as I write this book, I can honestly say, it is still a process. I'm learning to accept my body image and love myself even more, which hasn't always been easy. I have my share of stretch marks and cellulite. I have discoloration in my skin. I'm not the typical "model body", as I am an average African American woman whose weight has fluctuated throughout my life. I have always been very insecure about my breasts; I just didn't think they were pretty enough. I struggled with my weight so much that in high school, I felt it was a curse. The battle with my weight sent me into depression. I was either eating too much or too little. This was not healthy. The pressure to be thin was very strong. This was because the guys I liked the most only dated girls that were slim and petite. I wondered how I would measure up, being an average size 10/12 in my teens. I was scared that the worst would happen, that the guys I really liked would compare me to their exes and wish I was as small as they were. Over time,

I dated a couple guys that did not compare me to their ex-girlfriends, however, they wanted me smaller when I gained weight. This affected my self-esteem, causing me to question, *Would my husband love my body while pregnant with our children? Will he desire my body, even after having our children?* When it came to my body, I felt like a failure. I felt that I wouldn't measure up for any man, especially my future husband. But let me encourage you, that the man God has for YOU, will love YOU, FOR YOU! He will love and accept your body and see your "flaws" as beautiful.

I assure you by faith and knowing what I know from married women that have a real godly man in their lives: the one you will marry will desire you before, during pregnancy, and after you have your children. I want to reach at least one girl who may be feeling that way about her body, because I struggled so much, especially in my teens, and also, well into my twenties. I still affirm myself and tell myself while looking in the mirror that I have an amazing body. Affirmations are very helpful. My outlook about my body is still improving but has transformed so much already that I can't wait to see my confidence grow even more.

Even though I was never professionally diagnosed, I had close friends and family tell me that I suffered from body dysmorphia. Body Dysmorphic Disorder is a mental illness involving obsessive focus on a perceived flawed appearance. I was such a huge critic of my body. Even at the proper weight (for my height, 150lbs, or a size 8/9) I still felt I needed to lose another 20-30 pounds. Even then, I didn't feel I was small; I still thought something was wrong with me and that no one would want me at that size. I look back now having a healthy body image mindset (and many pounds later), and realize that I was a perfect size for me. I look at my photos from ages 15-19, where I worked on my health journey and fluctuated with my weight, and see that I was "good." I want to encourage you that if you are heavier than I was, don't roll your eyes and say my battle wasn't real, because it was. The struggle of not being healthy mentally concerning my body was torment. The thoughts of anorexia crossed my mind when I would throw up (due to being sick) and I would hop on the scale afterwards to see if I lost weight. I'm saddened that I went through that, and I am praying for any girl who is suffering with anorexia/bulimia. By the blood of Jesus, I declare that bondage is broken, IN JESUS NAME!

Now to all my hairy girls. Those with thick eyebrows, with uni-brows; those with facial hair, such as chin hairs, beards, mustaches; those with hairy arms, hairy legs, chest hair, and etc. I was extremely insecure about my facial hair and I began waxing my mustache and chin hairs, when I was fifteen years old. I was so embarrassed, and I still have to wax these areas to this very day. It was a major deal with my self-esteem (which I will discuss more in the next chapter). Even though I later found that due to high testosterone, I have PCOS (Polycystic Ovary Syndrome), which can cause weight gain, depression, and unwanted facial hair. I want to encourage all my sisters that feel defeated because of unwanted hair on your body, that you are still loveable and beautiful. Do the best you can to minimize it if it makes you self-conscious, but understand, your gender was not a mistake. You are well loved and accepted by God. I want to encourage the girl who is looking for validation in a man. Know that God is the only One that can validate you. Only Jesus can give your heart the deepest inner longing that you've been desiring and seeking!

Journal #2 Body Image

1. If God was to change one part of your body, what would you want it to be?
2. How long have you struggled with that particular body part?
3. How can you have peace about it if God never changes it?

_____

_____

_____

_____

_____

_____

_____

43

Chapter 3 Self-Esteem

According to the Merriam Webster Dictionary, self-esteem is the confidence and satisfaction in oneself: *self-respect*. For a very long time, I struggled with self-respect. I thought I loved myself, but I really didn't. When you have self-respect, confidence and satisfaction in yourself, you won't allow the pressures of the world to determine your worth. You won't allow the negativity from your peers to affect you because you are a child of God. You understand that God loves you and that you are royalty and part of His royal priesthood. You know you were worth dying for because Christ paid the price for you. Therefore any feelings of unworthiness are direct lies from the enemy. The devil knows that if he can ruin your self-esteem, he can take away your destiny. He will always make you feel incompetent and make you feel like you don't have the skills and qualifications to do what God has called you to do. The enemy always lies and tells you that you are not good enough.

If you fell victim to the traps of the enemy, then you are not alone. I fell victim to the trap *way* too many times.

As a minister of the Gospel, I can share with you that I've felt many times that

I was unworthy to hold this platform. I felt that because I fell short so many times (due to sin) that I automatically deserved Hell, not redemption and Grace. But the more I read God's Holy word, He showed me that my worth was in Him. A part of that worth is to know that His Grace and redemption are included. The Grace and redemption that God provides gives us the confidence that we need to get through this life and to connect deeper with God. I want to encourage you to let no one belittle you in any way. Your godly self-esteem cannot afford anyone who will tear down your self-worth. If these people are in your life, immediately cut them loose. I've learned that the longer you stay around people who don't have your best interest at heart, the more they will drain you. They take, but never give. The Bible declares that we are like eagles, and eagles soar high and never aim low to hang with pigeons. I want to ask you, who have you been hanging around that doesn't understand the high price that you are worth? I'm not telling you to go around being prideful or boastful and feel like you are better than others, or to look down on others. What I am saying is that life is too short to hold onto poison. People who are poisonous usually have a low self-esteem and don't really love themselves. They are miserable, so they want you to feel the same.

I had a friend who was very insecure in who she was. She would always talk about people who were bigger than she was. She was a petite woman. She always pointed out the flaws of others. The Lord began to minister to me that she did that because she had low self-esteem and she belittled others to make herself feel good. Sis, I want to encourage you right now that if you are always finding fault in other women, then it's time to stop and repent. We are all made in Christ's image. We should be building each other up and esteeming one another. I remember being on Facebook one day and saw a video of a dark-skinned girl in her class who said that she hated herself and didn't think she was pretty enough. After pouring out how she felt, the girls in her class surrounded her and hugged her and let her know how beautiful she was inside and out. It reminds me of God and His angels; we pour out to God our feelings and He sends His angels or tells us Himself how He really feels about us and who we are in Him. I want to encourage you, sis, that no matter what complexion or ethnicity you are, God designed you that way on purpose. No matter what society says, you are fearfully and wonderfully made, and God looks at you as good. You are altogether beautiful, and there is no flaw in you (Song of Solomon 4:7). You are more than your looks, and please know that looks do fade. Trust and know that true confidence comes from within and tapping into what God put into you.

You may look at celebrities and supermodels and think they have the best self-esteem and confidence, but most of them are hiding behind fame, drugs, sex, and alcohol. Sis, be a supermodel for Jesus! Let your light shine and show the world that it is possible by faith to have self-respect and confidence within oneself. If anything you do, let it be for the glory of God. If you are losing weight to build your self-esteem, do it for the glory of God, that you want to take care of your temple. If you are trying to gain weight, do it for the glory of God. In all that we do with ourselves, let's choose to honor Jesus. If you enjoy wearing makeup, wear it to enhance your beauty, not because it's what you think makes you beautiful. If no one told you today that you are beautiful, I want you to know from the bottom of my heart, you absolutely are, just the way you are!

Whether you decide to wear wigs, a weave, a perm, go natural, straightened or a 'fro, who said beauty and style had to come in one form? I'm natural and I had my last perm nine years ago. Through the journey I learned how to love me *naturally* just how God made me. I decided to find out, was I truly confident with my natural beauty? Or was I going to run back and get a perm, thinking only straight hair is beautiful? I needed to embrace my kinks and coils and be confident in them. It was a personal choice because since I was a little girl, I had super-curly hair and I longed for straight hair. It's funny how now I wish my texture was how it was before the perm, back super-curly again, but now I make it work with curling custards and creams. It's funny how now there are so many natural movements to say hey, natural beauty is beautiful, too. The reason why I emphasized my natural hair journey is because a lot of people tend not to find it as beautiful in comparison to wearing weaves, wigs, being permed, or having it straightened. I feel natural hair movements are breaking the norm, which is a good thing. In all, whatever you decide to rock, uplift every woman in the world and her choice of hairstyle and embrace how you were made! God loves you and sees you as truly a diamond. Rare and immaculate, you are!

Journal #3 Self-Esteem

1. Rate your self-esteem from 1-10, #1 being the lowest and #10 is the highest.
2. Do you find yourself comparing yourself to other women and/or superstars?
3. In what ways can you build your self-esteem (i.e. the word of God, List 10 positive things about yourself, etc.)?

_____

_____

_____

_____

Chapter 4 But I Thought He Was the One

It's been seven years since my last relationship ended, and all I can say it's been seven years of completion. Seven years of inner healing, growing my self-esteem, my confidence, being made whole, and most importantly, pursuing my purpose. Have I honestly thought I met the ONE before? Umm...well, at fifteen, I thought a guy was my future husband, but now, looking back, it was only a strong like. We never dated, but I continued to strongly like him, even when I dated my then boyfriends. I thought it was strange to be kissing my ex-boyfriend and wishing it was my first real crush I'd been kissing. When I dated my now-ex-boyfriends, I knew neither one of them were the ONE, but I entertained them because I thought, *I'm seventeen, I should have a boyfriend.* God told me with the first boyfriend to not date him and I did anyway. With my second boyfriend, God told me that I wasn't his wife and that we should only be friends for a season. I ignored God both times…how rebellious was I! I was heartbroken both times, but the second time stung the worst. I think when I got out of the relationship, I couldn't believe how one-sided it had been, I had hung on for far too long. I learned it's easier to date out of convenience and comfort than to focus on self-love and wait on God.

There were men who crossed my path during my seven years of being single, but my discernment grew and I wanted to obey God. For once, I wanted to give God full control over my life and trust Him for His very best for my life. I know many women wonder if the guy they are with is the one, but sis, let me encourage you: be with someone who honors God and honors His word. Be with someone who will make you better in Christ and who loves you unconditionally, like Christ loves the church. Be with someone who won't sin against you and God by engaging in sexual activity before marriage. Be with a man who won't try to control you or manipulate you or play mind games with you. Follow God, sis; He will give you wisdom and discernment to know how to pick a godly mate. You must develop a good relationship with God first; trust His voice and obey it. There are so many godly relationships that you see through social media, you may have some examples in your family (or maybe not). Trust that if marriage is your portion, God will bless you with an awesome marriage that glorifies Him.

I'm praying for you, sis. I've seen so many go down a path of putting a relationship together that God was not involved in. I've watched women settle for less than God's best because of impatience, loneliness, and sadness. For a long time I thought if God just blessed me with a man that truly loved me then I would be the happiest woman on Earth. I only wanted to feel accepted and loved. I wanted to be seen to someone as precious. I wanted to know that I was worthy to be loved. As uncomfortable as I felt, God began to show me that I needed to value me, in which I will talk about in the next chapter.

Journal #4 But I Thought He Was the One

1. Have you ever dated a guy and thought he was the ONE? Describe the experience.
2. What did you learn through that experience? Do you catch yourself dating the same type of man again?
3. List some traits you would like in the ONE (personality, looks, character, height, complexion, etc., list them all). Do you believe God can give you the desires of your heart? If not meditate and write this scripture down: Psalm 37:4.

Chapter 5 Value Me

The most difficult thing that I had to overcome and learn about myself was how to value me. I had to learn how to love myself and to recognize my own worth without relying on the validation of a man. I had to truly allow God to hold me on those nights where I cried myself to sleep due to loneliness. When I wanted to be deeply loved by a man I had to rely on the Lord. I came to understand that God truly cares about me and loves me. I needed to feel the warmth of the Holy Spirit. There were so many distractions coming my way, including men in whom I wanted to give my attention to. I was tested on several occasions to try and put my own thing together during my seven years of singleness. It was literally God's protection that pulled me through. I thought God was trying to torture me in my singleness. I didn't truly appreciate the gift of singleness until my eyes were opened in 2018. For seven years, I was on and off with my contentment in God. I will be the first to admit that I had more discontented times than contented. I felt like even though I so badly desired to be a wife, I didn't truly understand the effort and commitment that goes into marriage. I conversed with many wives who started to share with me their experiences.

Being a wife is a beautiful and huge responsibility.

When you are in your singleness, all you can think of is, *I'd rather have that than deal with my negative emotions, such as loneliness as a single.* When God has purposed you in your singleness, you must trust that He knows what's best for you. This builds other fruits of the spirit in your life as well. I had to learn how to have patience and self-control, and focus on the joy of the Lord. I now know that God values and loves me deeply. And in due season, HE will send a godly man my way who will love me the way God loves me. Jesus had to build confidence within me so that no one could ever tear me apart again. He wanted to show me my worth as a single person. I am worth more than rubies and as precious as gold. He wanted to build and strengthen me as a woman of God and that despite my illness, I am not deemed as unlovable. I have been rejected by men, but I take comfort in knowing that God still sees me as precious and as loveable.

I want to encourage you to know your worth in Christ. You are His most prized possession! He didn't allow what you went through to break you, but to build you. I know firsthand that I wouldn't be able to minister to you through writing this book if I didn't go through the process of struggling with my self-esteem. I am still on my journey, but by God's grace, I am in a much better place than I have ever been. Discovering my worth through the Word of God I have been able to release the negativity I felt about myself for years. I have been washed by Jesus' blood and He made me anew. Knowing that I'm a new creature in Christ has helped me seek after Christ even more. I realize how valuable I really am. My value is so high that I don't have to give free samples of myself to men. As I stay chaste in my singleness, I am learning to wait on the Lord.

It's by the grace of God that I can still say that I am a virgin. It was definitely not easy. This is not to make anyone feel bad that is not a virgin, but only to give hope to the teens and young adults, even mature adults that are virgins and still waiting. You are not alone, and the wait is worth it. For those who may say, *Sheree, that's not my testimony*, you can repent and wait for marriage as well. Just because you gave yourself to someone doesn't disqualify you from being worth the wait. You are still seen as precious to God even if you are mom with child(ren). You are so precious. Be an example for your children to follow. Following God's plan for sexual purity was never to deprive us but to save us from soul ties, unwanted pregnancy, sexually transmitted diseases, and much more. Just know that if that man calls himself a MAN of GOD, then he will respect you by honoring your temple for the Lord as well as his own temple. YOU ARE WORTH THE WAIT, SIS! Your past or present doesn't define you. You can move forward and get all that God has for you. You can find happiness in

Christ. Yes, the joy of the Lord can be your strength! God can give you self-control to honor your temple for the Lord.

He can give you the patience with yourself to see yourself as how God sees you. You are his beloved. He can restore you from your past. You do not deserve to be emotionally, verbally, physically, abused by anyone. You deserve the best that God has to offer! You can break the bad cycles in your life, you can break the generational curses and habits that you may have witnessed. You have worth. Jesus paid for that worth 2,000 years ago on the cross for you. You are worth more than being manipulated by someone who is immature. Let those toxic relationships go! Value yourself enough to love yourself fully. Value yourself enough to heal internally completely.

As you journey on, do not devoid yourself of attending counseling and therapeutic sessions. This is a first step which will help heal from an unkind past and learn how to work on loving yourself even the more. You are worth investing into. Therapy and counselling sessions are good for all ages. Therapy has proved beneficial for me and my inner healing. Find a trusted counselor and there is nothing wrong with seeking professional help. The best gift you can give yourself is loving and valuing yourself. Make yourself feel great and be great in the Lord so you can attract the same. Be the best you can be in Jesus. Find contentment in the Lord. God loves you! I love you, sis! You can make it! I promise God's plans towards you are good. Look up Jeremiah 29:11 right now and read it in every version out loud.

Journal #5 Value Me

1. What does Jeremiah 29:11 state and what does it mean to you?
2. How long have you noticed that you haven't valued yourself like you should? What are some ways you can improve that?
3. How do you view yourself? Do you see yourself as whole without a man?
4. How can you improve yourself to be more whole? Are you willing to go to therapy? If not, what makes you afraid of therapy and how can you work on that perspective about it?

Declaration to LOVE GOD

Mark 12:30 **New International Version**

Love the Lord your God with all your heart and with all your soul and with all your mind and with all your strength.

I,

_____

_____, vow to love God with my whole heart, soul, mind, and with all my strength. I give myself to Him whole heartedly with my mind, body, and spirit. I vow to spend time with Him daily, and get to know Him through His Word, the Bible, prayer, and by listening to worship music. I vow to attend Church regularly and get involved as it is related to my purpose, gifts, and talents. I vow to give of my resources to the kingdom of God so that it may in turn advance. I vow to worship God in spirit and in truth. I vow to put God first before anything. He has my heart, mind, body, and soul. I see Jesus as the lover of my soul and the apple of my eye. I vow to act, talk, and walk like Jesus. I vow to mirror my life after Jesus' life with God's help. In Jesus' name, Amen.

Signature of Witness & Date

My Signature & Date

Declaration to LOVE MYSELF

Song of Solomon 4:7 English Standard Version (ESV)

⁷ You are altogether beautiful, my love;

there is no flaw in you.

I, _____,

vow to love myself and to see myself how God sees me. I vow to speak positive things over myself and about myself to myself and others all the time. I vow to value myself and to teach other girls how to do the same. I vow to engage in activities to build my self-esteem daily. I vow to not entertain or involve myself with negative friendships and relationships. I vow to see myself as fearfully and wonderfully made. I vow to find my worth in God, not people, material things, status, etc. I vow to take care of my body for it is the temple of the Lord. I vow to love the skin I'm in. I vow to see myself as someone worthy to be loved. I vow to break from negative cycles that I or my family constantly repeats and start new cycles in Christ. I vow to purposely love my body image and everything that I see as a flaw. I vow to speak affirmations about myself and find the good things about me. I vow not to compare my life to another person's beauty, body, possessions, and status and/or material things. I vow to be content with who I am in Christ, my life, and my portion. In Jesus name, Amen.

_____

Signature of Witness & Date

_____

My Signature & Date

Declaration to wait for my future husband

Psalm 27:14 English Standard Version (ESV)

[14] Wait for the Lord; be strong, and let your heart take courage; wait for the Lord!

I, _____, vow to wait on my future husband. I vow not to entertain men who do not have a purpose for our relationship. I vow to save myself for marriage and to not have pre-marital sex until my wedding night. I vow to wait on God's very best for my life…a man who is a man after God's own heart. I vow to surrender my love life to the Lord. I vow not to awaken love before it is time. I vow to wait on the Lord for Him to present one of His sons to me. I vow to give my desires to the Lord and trust that He will blow my mind away with the best presentation for a spouse. I vow to believe the Lord and trust Him concerning my love life and it's in HIS hands. In Jesus' name, Amen.

Signature of Witness & Date

My Signature & Date

Note from Author

I hope you enjoyed reading this book as much as I did writing it. My heart's desire is to see young girls and women uplifted! The task of sharing my journey was not easy but I'm so glad I did. The experience has set me free and I pray that it will do the same for you. Take courage in knowing that God loves you immensely and that He is going to reveal so much to you. You are a living testimony of what someone needs to meet, see, hear, or read from. I hope you can feel my air hug through this book to you. As sisters, we can relate, as I know how it feels to go through the journey of self-esteem issues. We can overcome and conquer unhealthy self-esteem through Christ who strengthens us. I wish I would have read a self-esteem book when I needed it the most—in middle school, high school, and during college. Thank God I have read a couple of books along with the Word of God, to overcome my insecurities in which inspired me to share my struggles in such a way that youth and women of all ages can relate.

It is my prayer that you were blessed. If so, please feel free to email me at shereebraswell@gmail.com. Feel free to follow me on social media, facebook.com/sheree.p.braswell (Sheree B), Instagram: @sheree.p.braswell, twitter: @shereepbraswell!

I would love to hear from you!

About the Author

Sheree is a woman after God's own heart. She has a genuine love for God and for people. She is a mental health awareness advocate and serves at God's House of Deliverance Church, under the tutelage of Apostle Dr. Martina Wade-Hill. She is an inspirational speaker, ordained evangelist/elder, and intercessor. She is humbled by her experiences in life and is very transparent in her blog (www.shereebraswell.com) about her journey with Christ, living with a mental illness, education, self-esteem and singleness. Sheree has a passion and heart to see people be made whole and be set free.

She loves empowering and uplifting people with the word of God and speaking life into them, especially women and the youth. Sheree has a heart for missions work and to evangelize among those who are seeking to get to know the Lord, personally.

Sheree received her Associates Degree from Schoolcraft College in Communications and is a student at Eastern Michigan University in the Bachelors in Communications program minoring in Family Sociology. Sheree's goals are to receive her masters and become a marriage and family therapist.

Sheree enjoys reading, spending time with close family and friends. She also likes to hang out and laugh with them. She has a love for Zumba also.

ABOUT THE BOOK

All That Glitters Ain't Gold- A Guide for Every Girl to be Godly Esteemed is an invitation for every girl to dig deep into their lives and be esteemed no matter what chapter they are in their life. In this book, Sheree challenges you to find your worth and value in Christ and learn how to find confidence in Him. Be prepared to journal and feel as if you are having authentic girl talk with Sheree. She will impart her wisdom to you about having a godly self-esteem, relationships, and knowing more about yourself in Christ as far as your purpose is concerned. Get ready to feel the passion, warmth and love from Sheree as she shares her personal journey with having self-esteem to being godly-esteemed. Her prayer is that every lady will be blessed as she completes the book. Each reader will be left with a feeling of being a changed and renewed woman just as Sheree has experienced. This book is appropriate for all ages including very young girls to the mature grown woman. Through this book, you will smile and nod your head as Sheree shares her experiences and will be able to relate. You will find gold nuggets of wisdom as you journey through this book. As a bonus, Sheree includes vows that you can make to yourself, the Lord and your future husband! Get ready to feel golden!

Made in the USA
Middletown, DE
09 August 2019